NO NONSENSE NOTARY TRAINING

N.J. State Specific Notary Public Training

ALICE TULECKI

iUniverse, Inc.
Bloomington

No Nonsense Notary Training
N.J. State Specific Notary Public Training

Copyright © 2013 Alice Tulecki

iUniverse books may be ordered through booksellers or by contacting:

iUniverse
1663 Liberty Drive
Bloomington, IN 47403
www.iuniverse.com
1-800-Authors (1-800-288-4677)

ISBN: 978-1-4759-7797-4 (sc)
ISBN: 978-1-4759-7798-1 (e)

Printed in the United States of America

iUniverse rev. date: 5/1/2013

DISCLAIMER

The information contained in this program intended for instruction and guidance only. Alice Tulecki is a seasoned N.J. Notary Public, Commissioned Twenty One years at the time this manuscript was being first published.

The contents of this pamphlet may not be distributed, copied, or duplicated without the permission of Alice Tulecki, Documents & Professionals Services, LLC.

N.J. Notaries Public are not attorneys licensed to practice law in the State of New Jersey, and may not give legal advice.

(Ref. Opinion No. 41 – NJ Notary Public Manual; "Notaries Public and the Unauthorized Practice of Law N.J.S.A. 52:7-10 to 57:7-21.)

No Nonsense Notary Training

This New Jersey Notary Public Handbook designed for easy understanding – while pointing out the responsibilities, accountability and official action of your duties.

"The Office of the Notary Public is one of extreme Public Trust."

You have taken an OATH/AFFIRMATION mandated by legislative statute to perform your duties to clients and yourself "to the fullest extent of the law".

(Please feel free to email me at: alice.tulecki@gmail.com or visit the www.NotaryEducationforNJ.com and leave a message should you have a question.

D&PS strongly suggest that you have a Notary Membership with an educational source. We suggest ASN (American Society of Notaries).

N.N.N.T. came into existence because of the great need for N.J. Notaries Public to be educated on facts that are not covered in the N.J. Manual and are important for you to do your job professionally and with accuracy. The 2010 final version included suggestions from N.J.N.A Members: Jean Persut, Diana Brown and Patrica McGill – Parliamentary; The American Society of Notaries offered suggestions and approval.

References taken from the following resources and are reflected with initials: Van Alstyne's Notary Public Encyclopedia – VANPE; Model Notary Act - MNA; American Society of Notaries – ASN; – NJ Notary Public Manual – NJNPM.

MY NOTES:

_____

_____

_____

_____

_____

_____

_____

_____

This insert is an attempt to impress upon NEW JERSEY NOTARIES PUBLIC the importance of the "OATH" and "AFFIRMATION". We the public, in our daily life, are not exposed to the everyday occurrence of: hearing or using the words: "OATH" &/or Affirmation", or even understand what they TRULY mean. (Not A FAX to SIGN & SEAL.)

The American Heritage Dictionary states:

"OATH"
a) A solemn, formal declaration or <u>promise </u>to fulfill a pledge, often calling upon God or a god as witness. b) The words or formula of such a declaration or promise. c) Something that is promised or declared.
<u>**"PROMISE"**</u>
a) Declaration assuring that one will or will not do something. "VOW".
b) A pledge or offer of assurance.
"VOW"
An earnest promise or pledge that binds one to perform a specific act.

"AFFIRMATION"
a) Maintaining "TRUTH". b) To ratify or confirm. Affirming or asserting that something is true or factual.

N.J. State Constitution 1947

OATH/AFFIRMATION OF OFFICE
Updated, through amendments adopted in November, 2011.

Article IV,   Section VIII   NJ CONSTITUTION

"Every officer of the Legislature shall, before he enters upon his duties, take and subscribe the following oath or affirmation: "I do solemnly promise and swear (or affirm) that I will faithfully, impartially and justly perform all the duties of the office of: _____, to the best of my ability and understanding; <u>"that I will carefully preserve all records, papers, writings, or property entrusted to me for safekeeping"</u> by virtue of my office, and make such disposition of the same as may be required by law."

Notary Public 1979 - New Jersey Statutes Annotated
52:7-14. Oath; filing; certificate of commission and qualification.

Within 3 months of the receipt of his/her commission, each notary public shall take and subscribe an oath before the clerk of county in which he resides, <u>faithfully and honestly to discharge the duties of his office, and that he will make and keep a true record of all such matters as are required by law,</u> which oath shall be filed with said clerk. The oath of office of a nonresident notary public shall be taken and subscribed before the clerk of the county in which he maintains his office or is employed in this State.   L. 1979, c. 460, § 5.

It is, assumed if you are studying this handbook, you are interested in being a far-sighted New Jersey Notary Public. Documents & Professional Services strongly suggest it is to your benefit to affiliate with a Notary Public organization that offers you training and a hotline to answer your questions. It is not in your best interest to have the DOCUMENT PROVIDER advise you.

Please report any errors you find in this handbook. Any errors were an oversight; and will be addressed accordingly.

Before your first notarization, please note the following:

Read the N.J. Notary Manual.

READ & Print "OPINION 41".

Use Resources – provided.

Become a member of a Notary Public organization.

Take out an E&O policy.

Understands the differences of:
a. Acknowledgement
b. Jurat
c. Affidavit

MY NOTES:
_____
_____
_____
_____
_____
_____
_____
_____

Table Of Contents

Section I
The Office of the Notary Public

MY OPENING NOTES AND QUESTIONS ....PAGE 7

Practice of Office　　　　　　　　　　　　　　8 - 12
What Is a Notary Public
Legal Liability
Advertising
Unauthorized Practice of Law
Foreign Language
Disqualification
Common Errors

Fees/Oats/Affirmations　　　　　　　　　　　　13

What a Notary is prohibited from doing　　　　14

Bank of America　　　　　　　　　　　　　　　15

Tools of the Trade　　　　　　　　　　　　16-19
Rubber/Wet Stamp
Journal
Notary Certificates
Embosser
Finger Print Device
I.D. Guide
E&O Insurance - Continuing Education
Notary Public Membership
My Section Notes 19

Section II
Guidelines for Notarial Services

Execution of Duties　　　　　　　　　　　　20-22
Jurisdiction / Term of Office
Authorization To Do and Conflict of Interest
Identification
My Section Notes.......................,,,,,,,,,,,,,,,,,,,,,..............22

Table Of Contents

Section III
Guidelines for Notarial Services

Parts of the Certificate   **23-31**
        Parts/Illustrations
        Acknowledgement
        Jurat
        Affidavit
        Oaths & Affirmations
        Apostilles & Authentication
        Banking – Protest/ Safe Deposit Box

        Section 3 Notes Page………………………………………**32**

Section IV
Tips for the Notary Public

Knowledge is Power   **33**
Getting Started   **34**
Following Completion   **35-36**
    Support - Contacts - Supplies – Membership
    And Valuable Resources

Section V
The New Notary Public

The Pro Active Notary Public   **37-43**
    Reads the N.J. Notary Public Manual
    READS & PRINT OPINION 41
    Uses resources – contact information provided
    Has a Notary Public Organization Membership
    READS & PRINT OPINION 41
    Takes out an E&O Policy
    Understand the differences between – Acknowledgements – Jurats – Affidavits

    My Section 4 and 5 Notes………………………………………… **38**
    Sample – All Purpose Acknowledgement – Jurat – Affidavit   **39-41**
Counties Directory   **42**

MY Opening NOTES and Questions:

_____

_____

_____

_____

_____

_____

_____

_____

_____

_____

_____

_____

_____

_____

_____

_____

_____

_____

_____

_____

Section 1
THE OFFICE OF NOTARY PUBLIC
PRACTICE OF OFFICE

WHAT IS A NOTARY PUBLIC

➢ The Notary Public is the "First Responder" in preventing fraud.....by positively identifying the signers via "satisfactory evidence".

➢ A Notary Public is a sworn public and state officer who serves as an impartial witness to the signing of documents and to the acknowledgement of signatures on documents.

➢ A notary public is a public official whose powers and duties are defined by statute.

➢ A N.J. notary public is a public servant with statewide jurisdiction and authorized to take acknowledgments, protest instruments permitted by law to be protested, administer oaths, and take depositions.

➢ Each Notary Public takes an official oath of office "to faithfully perform" the duties of the office and to protect the information of their signers.

➢ The primary duty of a Notary Public is as a disinterested witness. He/She duly notifies the signer of an instrument as to the importance of such document, and the signer of such document, declares that the signer's identity, signature, and reasons for signing such instrument are genuine.

➢ The signature and seal of a Notary Public provide proof of these facts and allow persons in trade and commerce to rely upon the truth and veracity of the Notary Public as a third party who has no personal interest in the transaction.

➢ A Notary Public is personally liable for negligence or fraud in the performance of the duties of the office. In addition to civil liability, Notaries Public may be subject to criminal prosecution and the revocation or suspension of their notary public commission by the Treasurer's office.

MY NOTES:

_____

_____

_____

_____

_____

LEGAL LIABILITY:

- **Liability – Notaries are *ministerial officials. Notaries generally may be held financially responsible for all damages caused by their mistakes or misconduct in performing notarial acts. Possible penalties include but may not be limited to: being sued in civil court and ordered to pay all resulting damages, including attorney fees.**
- **Bonds – Not required**
- **E&O Insurance –**
  - **Not required by State Of New Jersey – Highly recommended to cover legitimate errors on your Notarial Certificates.**
  - **According to M.N.A. Ref. 13-1. The EMPLOYER IS LIABLE FOR ALL DAMAGES caused by the notary's negligence, and/or misconduct in performing a notarization during employment.**
- **BOA vs. Ross E. Bird doc.#5-08-0188; Appellate Court of IL, 5th Dist. Results: *Employers of Notaries MUST Train and Supervise or FACE DIRECT LIABILITY FOR FAILURE TO PREVENT HARM TO THIRD PARTIES. February 2009. This supports the M.N.A.***
- **D&PS highly recommends E&O Insurance. E&O Insurance will absorb a Notary's expenses in defending against a lawsuit caused by a Notary's unintentional mistake up to the limit of the policy. Errors excluded from coverage caused by a notary's violation of state law or commission fraud. The BEST form of insurance for notaries is PROPER EDUCATION, TRAINING, KNOWING THE LAW AND PROCESS; CAREFUL COMPLETION OF THE NOTARIAL CERTIFICATE WITH UTMOST ACCURACY AND INTEGRITY; NOT GIVING INFORMATION REGARDING DOCUMENTS BEING SIGNED.**
- **Willful violations such as fraud and dishonesty can lead to removal of the Notary's commission, and leave the Notary vulnerable to civil and/or criminal legal actions. N.J.S.A. 2C:43-3.**
- **In the capacity of a Notary, acting as a legal advocate "is considered" the unauthorized practice of law (Ref. Opinion 41).**

> *** Ministerial: According to the American Heritage Dictionary ministerial means:**
>   i. **Of or pertaining to administrative and executive duties or functions of government.**
>   ii. **LAW – Of or designating a mandatory act or duty admitting of no personal discretion or judgment in its performance.**
>   iii. **Acting or serving as an agent; instrumental.**

MY NOTES:

_____

_____
_____
_____
_____
_____

ADVERTISING:

False or Misleading Advertising:
A Notary's commission "may be revoked or suspended for making claims or advertising powers not authorized by law". Practicing fraud or deceit in advertising or other activity as a Notary Public maybe found guilty of a crime of the second degree or above. (N.J.S.A. 2C:21-31).

Translating "Notary Public" into Spanish:
Notaries abroad, commissioned under the civil law system, have expanded powers than America's common-law notaries. Many foreign notaries are attorneys.

An American notary's use of the term "notario publico" or "notaria publica" could mislead persons from other countries to believe that the U.S. notary has the power similar to notaries abroad. Unscrupulous notaries have abused this misconception, primarily through advertising to defraud unsuspecting victims. In New Jersey, notaries using the term "notario publico" or "notaria publica" were accused of illegal advertising practices; subjected to removal from office.

Unauthorized Practice of Law

(Ref. Opinion 41, *N.J.S.A.* 2C:21-22 and *Rule* 1.21-1(a) governing the unauthorized practice of law, and compared with *N.J.S.A.* 52:7-10 to 52:7-21, the *Notaries Public, Act of 1979*).

N.N.N.T.'s research discloses that some notaries public in New Jersey are performing functions outside the scope permitted by statute. N.N.N.T. has concluded that to prevent future unauthorized practice of law and to give guidance to notaries public and unwary consumers it is necessary to define the role of a notary public. The goal of N.N.N.T. is to inform New Jersey Notaries Public the importance of following statutes; protecting the public and themselves. N.N.N.T. along with A.S.N. and N.N.A. promote education for notaries and the public.

MY NOTES:

_____
_____
_____
_____
_____
_____
_____
_____
_____

FOREIGN LANGUAGE:

Foreign-Speaking Signers:
There should always be direct communication between the Notary and document signer, whether in English or any other language. Never rely upon an interpreter. Misunderstanding can happen. (Ref. N.N.A.)

Foreign Documents:
Direct understanding of notarizations and documents, notaries and signer(s) must speak the language of the documents. There are difficulties and dangers for a notary notarizing a document that he/she "cannot understand".

Prerequisite to recording: (N.J.S.A. 46:15-1.1).
Any instrument affecting title to Real Estate will be recorded on presentation to the recording officer of any county in which all or part of the real estate is located; must be in ENGLISH or accompanied by a translation into ENGLISH.

DISQUALIFICATIONS:

1. Notarial Certificate requirements: (NJSA 2A:82-17, 46-2.1) MISSING All or part of:
   i. VENUE - STATEMENT/TESTIMONIUM – NOTARY
   ii. SIGNATURE – SEAL (mechanical not required): required: print, type, or stamp:
   iii. Notary name; should a seal be used suggested: Title of office (NP), Jurisdiction (NJ)
   iv. Commission expiration date.

2. Notarizes their own signature, or notarizes a transaction to which the notary is a party or has a financial or beneficial interest; is party to or named in the   document...ex witness signature.
3. Has Financial or Beneficial Interest by being named principal in a financial transaction; receives a financial advantage, right, privilege, property or fee in excess of lawful notarial fee.

MY NOTES:

_____
_____
_____
_____
_____
_____
_____
_____
_____

DISQUALIFICATIONS CONTINUED…

4. Notarizing for Relatives - State Officials strongly discourage notarizing for family, blood or marriage, domestic partner, step or half relatives, etc. One never knows when a benefit or financial gain may come into play, whether it be small or large. Sometimes this is a clear-cut disqualifying financial-beneficial interest- Spouse, friend or relative. Other times may be more difficult for the notary to be impartial.

5. State of N.J. Office of Notary Public; VANPE & N.J.N.A. recommend that N.J. Notaries NOT witness and notarize the same document. Few if any state addresses this common question. Some say the witness becomes part of the document and others say "NO" they do not. It is always better for the notary to side with common sense and good judgment in performing their duties.

6. If the notary is performing willful violations, such as fraud and dishonesty, this can lead to removal of the notary's commission.

7. A notary is <u>disqualified</u> from performing a notarization act if the notary: Is found to have a financial or other beneficial interest, witnesses and notarizes or notarizes own signature.

COMMON ERRORS

NO PERSONAL APPEARANCE

DOES NOT WITNESS THE SIGNATURE BEING SIGNED

FAILS TO GIVE OATH – AFFIRMATION

LETS OTHER USE EQUIPMENT

MY NOTES:

_____
_____
_____
_____
_____
_____
_____
_____
_____

Fees, Oaths, Affirmation and Acknowledgement

Notaries may charge only the statutory fee for administering an oath or affirmation NJSA 22A:4-14

1. Administering an Oath/Affirmation or taking an affidavit - $2.50
2. For taking proof of a deed - $2.50
3. For taking all acknowledgements - $2.50
4. Taking acknowledgements, of the grantors in the transfer of real estate, regardless of the number of such services performed, in a single transaction to transfer real estate - $15.00.
5. Taking acknowledgements of the mortgagors in the financing of real estate regardless of the number of such services performed in a single transaction to transfer real estate - $25.00.
6. There is no fee swearing in a witness in conjunction with an acknowledgment.

Oaths, Affirmations and Acknowledgements

"MUST BE ADMINISTERED VERBALLY"
AND
"RESPONDED TO IN THE POSITIVE"

- **OATH:** DO YOU SWEAR THAT THE INFORMATION PRESENTED IN THIS DOCUMENT ENTITLED "ABC", WHICH YOU HAVE SIGNED BEFORE ME, IS THE TRUTH, SO HELP YOU GOD. (N.J.S.A 41:2-17)

- **AFFIRMATION:** DO YOU AFFIRM THAT THE STATEMENTS PRESENTED IN THIS DOCUMENT ENTITLED "ABC", WHICH YOU HAVE SIGNED BEFORE ME, ARE THE TRUTH, THE WHOLE TRUTH AND NOTHING BUT THE TRUTH? (N.J.S.A. 41:1-6).

- **ACKNOWLEDGEMENT:** SIGNER MUST ACKNOWLEDGE SIGNATURE WAS MADE FREELY FOR THE PURPOSE INTENDED IN THE DOCUMENT. (N.J.S.A.46:14-2.1). Exception to appearance: When being notarized signer MUST acknowledge the signature is theirs and MUST APPEAR before notarization takes place.

MY NOTES:

_____

_____

_____

_____

WHAT IS A NOTARY PROHIBITED FROM DOING?

- Never pre-date an action. The Notary may never date an acknowledgement, Jurat, etc., prior to the execution of signature and date of appearing signer.
- NEVER – SIGN AND STAMP – INCOMPLETE NOTARIAL - LANGUAGE ALWAYS.
- Never lend a journal, stamp, or other personalized Notary equipment to another individual.
- Never prepare a legal document or give advice on legal matters, or matters pertaining to land titles. This includes the preparation of pleadings, affidavits, briefs and any other submissions to the court. (Opinion 41)
- Never, in the capacity as a Notary Public, appear as a representative of another person in a legal proceeding.
- Never, notarize documents without the physical presence of the signer.
- Notaries should refrain from notarizing documents in which they have a personal interest including documents they have prepared for a fee.
- Never notarize documents for relatives. Not LAW N.J. N.P. Manual strongly states.
- Never notarize your own signature. (DO NOT witness a document that you are notarizing.)
- Never imply you are anything more than what you are. EX. Attorney, Accountant.
- Never use the term: "NOTARIO PUBLICO", as this indicate something more than a Notary Public is allowed to do.
- Never certify a photograph, copies of public or foreign records.

MY NOTES:

_____
_____
_____
_____
_____
_____
_____
_____
_____

BANK OF AMERICA
• File #5-08-0188
• IN THE APPELLATE COURT OF ILLINOIS - FIFTH DISTRICT

This court case should make every N.J. Notary Public open their eyes.
The result was:

"EMPLOYERS ARE RESPONSIBLE FOR EDUCATING THEIR NOTARIES".

INDEPENDENT NOTARIES:
NEED TO PAY ATTENTION TO THIS IMPORTANT RULING.

GET YOURSELF EDUCATED

MY NOTES:

_____
_____
_____
_____
_____
_____
_____
_____

Tools of the Trade

1. **Rubber Stamp:** In addition to their signature, N.J. law requires N.J. Notaries Public print, type or stamp their name on every document notarized. N.J.S.A 52:7-19. The Notary Public Manual also requires that the Notary's commission expiration date be also printed, typed or stamped on each notarization.

2. **Journal:** Although, it is not the law in N.J. to keep a Journal book, NJSA 52:7-14 states: "When the notary takes an Oath before the clerk of the county h/she resides in, the notary should pay attention to the instruction of the "OATH". The Oath of Office states: *"h/she will make and keep a true record of all such matters as are required by law.* YOUR, Oath is filed by the county clerk. By Keeping a Journal, you will have a record that provides proof of identification, signature, thumbprint, date and place of notarization, kind of notarization, and a place for notes.

3. **Notarial Certificates:** It is a good idea to carry a supply of Jurats and Acknowledgements with you. (Never ever, just sign and seal without proper text or pre-stamp or sign notarial certificates.)

4. **Embosser:** A steel device used to place a raised seal on one or more documents. The seal, can be felt when touched. It is a means preventing someone from inserting other pages into a set of documents. D&PS suggest that if using an embosser, it be used on all notarial certificates. When an embosser is used for multiple pages fan the pages embossing of all certificates while enabling embossing on the multiple pages.

5. **Fingerprinting device:** Presently not required by law in New Jersey, but obtaining the signer(s) thumbprint is a strong deterrent against fraud. M.N.A. 7:3 states it is the ultimate proof that the signer appeared before the notary.

6. **Identification Guide:** Helps you identify driver's license, passport, and many other forms of identification that you are not familiar with.

7. **Error and Omissions Insurance:** It is highly recommended that you carry E&O insurance. These policies do not cover damages caused by the notary's violation of state law or commission fraud.

8. **Education: D&PS** highly recommends every Notary Public needs education and training. D&PS suggest that you should not take the direction from the document preparer. Guidance is always helpful, but, should be verified by a good notary source. It is your Commission and you can be fined – go to jail – lose your commission. Anyone or all of these reprimands could be fall you.

9. **MEMBERSHIP:** D&PS believes this is a great source for immediate information and growth. D&PS recommends ASN (American Society of Notaries).

MY NOTES:

_____

_____

_____

_____

_____

_____

_____

Official Seal (N.J.S.A. 41:1-7)

N.J. law does not require notaries to use wet seals of office. However, N.J.S.A. 52:7-19 specifically states that notaries are to: subscribe his/her signature to each Jurat/ Acknowledgement Impress his/her name by printing, typing, or by wet seal or mechanical stamp enabling the State Treasurer to easily read the name.

To Emboss "for" Fraud Prevention!

Not the law in N.J. but D&PS strongly suggests that an embosser be used. A great fraud prevention tool, it produces a raised seal on the document. If an embosser is used, it should be placed along the margin of a page(s) and not over wording.

We should note that the embosser is being used less and less. In the USA, the rubber stamp is being used and recognized in its place. However, Foreign Countries see the rubber stamp as "Phony". (Ref. VANPE)

Journal - Written Chronological Record

- D&PS strongly supports all Notaries keeping a journal of their notarial acts. Note: There is no specific law. The Oath (N.J.S.A. 52:7-14) we take before the clerk indicates that we will faithfully and honestly discharge the duties of office, and *we make and keep a true record of such matters.* The state highly recommends that a journal be kept.
- A well-kept journal shows that a Notary demonstrated reasonable care when notarizing, and provides important information if any questions are asked about a transaction.
- A journal entry also can provide valuable assistance to law enforcement in catching and prosecuting criminals in connection to a fraud or other crime.

MY NOTES:

_____
_____
_____
_____
_____
_____
_____
_____

Notary Certificates

Preprinted Acknowledgements – Jurats – use full to have extra supply in case of errors. *Never pre-sign or stamp certificates.*

Fingerprint Device

For further proof of identification, aids in fraud prevention. (Not the law in N.J.)

I.D. Guide

Glossary, showing the current forms of Drivers License, for each state. Passports and other forms of identification maybe included. Helpful, when presented with out of state driver's license and/or other acceptable identification.

E&O Insurance

Protection if a notary should be sued for damages resulting in unintentional errors and/or omissions on your Notarial Certificate. E&O insurance will not protect notary for intentional wrongdoing.

Notary Public Membership

A valuable resource when you need an answer immediately. Most memberships include advertising your business.

MY NOTES:

_____

_____

_____

_____

_____

_____

_____

_____

_____

MY NOTES: SECTION 1

<u>SECTION 2</u>

GUIDELINES FOR NOTARY SERVICES

Execution of Duties

Jurisdiction: Statewide. (N.J.S.A.52:7-15)

A duly commissioned and qualified notary is authorized to perform their duties throughout the state; can request from the clerk where qualified certificates of commission and qualification for filling with other county clerks within the state. The notary then will present them to the various clerks and provide their autograph signature for filing.

Term of Office: Five years. (N.J.S.A. 52:7-11)

Term begins on the date the State Treasurer puts on the certificate. Expiration ends at midnight of the date on the certificate or as deemed by the State Treasurer.

What is a Notary Authorized to do?

New Jersey State law authorizes a duly commissioned and sworn Notary to perform the following duties in any county in New Jersey:

Administer oaths, affirmations and affidavits (NJSA 41:2-1, 41:2-17).
Take acknowledgments and proofs (NJSA 46:14-6.1).
Execute protests for non-payment or non-acceptance NJSA 2A:82-7). (Rarely done)
Witnessing a Safe Deposit Box Opening (NJSA 17:14A-51).

Conflict of Interest

- By virtue of the notary's official position, the notary has a personal interest by law to perform the notarization objectively with integrity on behalf of the state of New Jersey.
- The notary's official position dictates "Impartiality" and "disinterest" as a witness.
- A notary is to have a high standard of principles and ethical conduct. Notarial conflicts between objective performance of official duties and the opportunity for personal gain from transactions on which the notarization is being performed.
- The notary must be mindful of the error of notarizing documents for relatives.
- The notary must be aware that they MUST not witness and notarize a document.
- The notary must be aware NOT to notarize their own signatures.

Identification

　　　Though states have been working diligently to create more secure, tamper-proof identification documents, criminals are always seeking new ways to evade or copy security measures. That is where Notaries come in. The Notary's personal diligence in establishing a signer's identity and willingness to sign a document through conversation, observation and questioning, along with a careful record of the transactions kept in the Notary's journal, is a vital step in protecting documents against possible fraud.

Identification to be recorded in your journal

Proof - N.J.S.A. 46:14-2.1 (2)

1. Acceptable Type of Identification - w/photo and signature; date of Expiration/issue/Birth/; weight/height/ eye color; address

Drivers License
US Passport
Foreign Passport stamped by INS
US Military ID
Personal Knowledge of signer

2. Unacceptable Type of Identification
Social Security Card
Credit Card
Temporary Drivers License or
Driver's license or other without photo

3) Personal Appearance is necessary. 46:14-2.1 (1)

Multiple Identifications

　　　As a Notary Public there may be times when you suspect possible deceit, ask for multiple forms of identification. Document all. Remember, you the notary public MUST be satisfied. If you are not, WALK AWAY…REMEMBER "keep yourself safe". What to look for in identification materials: Look for evidence of. Tampering, counterfeiting, mismatched type styles, photo that is raised, signature that does not match the document, smudges, erasures, smears, discolorations, misspelled words, new looking card with an old expiration date. Ask signer for DOB or some other I.D. shown or look for color of eyes…do they match?

MY NOTES: Section 2

SECTION 3

Parts of the Certificate

NOTE: ALL Single Notarial Certificates that are separated from the document and signature page should note similar notation: "This certificate is attached to a
_____ [title of document], dated _____ [date of document], regarding or concerning _____ [loan # or other pertinent information regarding the transaction], consisting of _____ pages (# of pages)."

ILLUSTRATIONS

      The following illustrations intended to show the basic elements of two common notary actions -- acknowledgments and jurats. The illustrations serve, AS EXAMPLES ONLY, not intended to be comprehensive or exclusive standards. N.J. Standard: Venue – Text – Notary Signature – Printed Name – Commission expiration date.

      (For Professional appearance and good notary practice a "Universal" wet seal that is photo-graphically reproducible, with: Notary Public, State of New Jersey, Name as it appears n commission, Commission Expiration date & Commission Number. More is better than less and the statute is open.)

N.J.S.A. 46:14-2.1 "<u>Acknowledgement</u>"

VENUE	= State of New Jersey - (where you are standing at the
VENUE	= County of Ocean)time the certificate is signed and wet sealed.
TEXT	= Date – signer(s) appear before you; Name of signer and Notary Public Name, Personally Appeared – Identification means
SIGNATURE	= Notary Public – MUST be signed as on your Notary Commission. Print name under signature.
SEAL	= Commission Expiration Date (Professional = D&PS recommend using a rubber stamp with: Name, Title, State, Commission number and expiration date.)

MY NOTES:

_____

_____

_____

_____

_____

Requirements for Taking an Acknowledgment
N.J.S.A. 46:14-2.1

Ensure that the <u>signer appears before the notary and presents at least one form of photo identification</u> that provides a physical description of the signer: photograph, DOB, DOI, DOE, Registration number,   e.g., driver's license or passport.

<u>Signer ACKNOWLEDGES that the signature was made freely for the purpose intended in the document.</u> N.J.S.A. 46:14-4.2 "Signers signature can be any mark made on the document by a person who intends to give legal effect to the document". Thereby, giving authority and intent.

D&PS strongly recommends that all notarial acts for an acknowledgment or an oath/affirmation be accompanied by the appropriate verbal ceremony; for example (acknowledgement), "Do you acknowledge signing this document willingly, for its stated purpose?

Note: Personal knowledge or satisfactory evidence of identification is required; <u>such evidence includes identification documents and/or oath of a credible witness.</u>

In executing an acknowledgment, a *Notary* <u>TAKES OR EXECUTES</u> an acknowledgment while a *document signer* <u>MAKES OR GIVES</u> an acknowledgment.

1. The SIGNER(S) MUST PERSONALLY appear to sign the document BEFORE THE NOTARY, at the time of the notarization.
2. The Notary watches the signature('s) being made at the time of the notarization.
3. Taking an acknowledgement: $2.50 per signature, per notarial certificate. N.J.S.A. 22A:4-14

<u>CERTIFICATE OF ACKNOWLEDGMENT</u>

The following illustration reflects the basic elements of a certificate of acknowledgment. The certificate wording "could be" incorporated into the document involved, or may be attached to the document as a separate sheet. Language or lines that do not apply to a particular action may be crossed out -- e.g., crossing out the words; "Witness(es)" when none appear.

MY NOTES:

_____

_____

_____

_____

_____

_____

All Purpose Acknowledgement

State of: New Jersey)

           (**WHERE YOUR FEET ARE PLANTED**

County of: Ocean   )

On this _____ day of _____, 20_____ before me
_____ _____, a
Notary Public personally appeared:
_____, ~~personally known to me~~ OR proved to me on the basis of satisfactory evidence to be the person/persons whose name/names is/are subscribed to the within instrument and acknowledged to me that he/she/they executed the same in his/her/their authorized capacity/capacities, and that by his/her/their signature/signatures on the instrument the person/persons acted, executed this instrument.

Witness my hand and seal: _____ _____,

                                                ^ Notary Public Signature -
                                              Printed name below line
                                              My Commission Expires:

Seal

NJSA 41:2.17   JURAT

A "jurat" is the notarial certificate for an oath/affirmation notarial act, for which the signer appearing before the notary swears (oath) or affirms (affirmation) that the contents of the document are true.

1. The SIGNER(S) MUST PERSONALLY appear to sign the document BEFORE THE NOTARY.
2. The Notary watches the signature('s) being made at the time of the notarization.
3. The Oath/Affirmation given to the Signer (s), Signer(s) must respond in the affirmative NJSA 41:2-17; $2.50 per signature, per notarial certificate.
NJSA 22A:4-14

VENUE   = Where you are standing at the time the certificate is signed and "sealed"
                 Ex. New Jersey   Ocean County
TEXT   = Subscribed/Signed and sworn/affirmed before Name of
                 Notary Public, Date signer(s) appeared before N.P. SIGNATURE =
                 Notary Public – MUST be signed as on your Notary Commission. Print
                 name under signature.
SEAL   = Commission Expiration date. Professional = D&PS recommend using a
                 rubber stamp with: Name, Title, State, Commission Number and
                 expiration date.

CERTIFICATE OFJURAT - N.J.S.A. 52:7-19

The following illustration reflects the basic elements of a Jurat. The certificate wording could be incorporated into the document involved, or may be attached to the document on a separate sheet. Language or lines that do not apply to a particular action may be crossed out -- e.g., crossing out the words, "~~Witness(es)~~" when none appear.

Jurat

State of: New Jersey)

　　　　　　　　　　　(WHERE YOUR FEET ARE PLANTED

County of: Ocean　　)

Subscribed and sworn or affirmed before me by _____, this _____ day of _____, 20_____.

Witness my hand and seal:　　　　　_____

　　　　　　　　　　　　　　　　　^ Notary Signature - Printed Name below line
　　　　　　　　　　　　　　　　　　　My Commission Expires:

　　　　　　　　　　　SEAL

CERTIFICATE OF AFFIDAVIT

An affidavit is a document containing a statement voluntarily signed and sworn to or affirmed before a notary or other official with oath-administering powers. (NJSA 41:2-17).

This document "could" be identified as a sandwich certificate. Its elements are: 1, Notary completes the Venue at the top of the affidavit. 2. Sandwiched in the middle would be the signer's written statement and signature.

VENUE　　　　= State of New Jersey - (where you are standing at
VENUE　　　　= County of Ocean　　　　)the time the certificate is signed and "sealed".
SIGNER　　　 = MAKES A STATEMENT
SIGNER　　　 = SIGNATURE

NOTARY COMPLETES THE JURAT AT THE BOTTOM.

TEXT　　　　　= Subscribed/Signed and sworn/affirmed before N.P. Date signer appear
　　　　　　　　before you followed by signers name.
SIGNATURE = Notary Public – MUST be as signed on commission.
SEAL　　　　 = Commission Expiration date. (Professional = D&PS recommend using
a rubber stamp with: Name, Title, State, and Commission number with expiration date.

CERTIFICATE OF AFFIDAVIT

State of New Jersey   **County Ocean**

I, John Smith, being duly sworn, make this my affidavit and state: _____
_____ (This section contains the written statement.) ex. My wife Mary
Smith has my permission to register my 2010 Ford Focus. I have signed, dated and
filled out all required information. As my wife should their an issue you have my
permission to re request she accommodate your inquiries. Thank you.   Etc….

_____
_____
_____

Affiant's Signature& date >>>   _____
                                           Print Name of Affiant

Subscribed and sworn to before me on _____ 20__, by _____.
                                                     (Affiant's name)

                                      _____ _____
                                           ^ Notary Signature Print below
                                           My Commission Expires: _____

                     Seal

MY NOTES:

_____
_____
_____
_____
_____
_____
_____

BLANK STATEMENTS

<u>NEVER</u> – <u>EVER</u> !

JUST SIGN AND STAMP

YOUR SIGNATURE ON A DOCUMENT

OR

STAMP OR PRINT ALONE..

MEANING: NO VENUE, DATE, TEXT =

GO TO JAIL
GET FINED
OR BOTH
AND
LOSE COMMISSION!

My Notes:

_____

_____

_____

_____

_____

Oaths and Affirmations

BY LAW MUST BE ADMINISTERED NJSA 41:2-17

An oath/affirmation is a spoken pledge, administered along with the affixation of the signature by a person appearing before the Notary.

An Oath is a solemn pledge to a Supreme Being.

An affirmation is a solemn statement without oath.

Note. Administering an oath or Affirmation is serious and MUST be given verbally.

The person swearing or affirming needs to acknowledge verbally in the positive "YES" or "I DO".

Both are promises of truthfulness and have the same legal effect. If one fails to be truthful, they may be subject to criminal penalties for perjury.

Whenever law requires an oath, an affirmation, may be taken instead. This accommodates persons who have conscientious objections against taking an oath (NJSA 41:1-6).

Notaries may administer oaths and affirmations to public officials and officers of various organizations; in executing jurats for affidavits/verifications and to swear in witnesses (N.J.S.A. 41:2-17).

EX. "Do you swear that the information presented in this document(s) which you are to sign before me, is the truth, so help you God?"

"Do you solemnly affirm that the information presented in this document(s) which you are to sign before me, is the truth, and this you affirm under the pains and penalties of perjury?"

My Notes:

_____

_____

_____

_____

_____

_____

_____

APOSTILLES - NJSA 52:7-15, 52:7-16

Apostilles, are often used in transactions, involving international documents and exchange, including adoption transactions. An Apostille, is provided, if the transaction involves a country that subscribes to the Hague Treaty. The Apostille is an additional document to be notarized from the state, to affirm that the notary has been duly commissioned, sworn in and provided a seal. The actual notarization requires an embossment with a colored, usually gold, seal.

To obtain an Apostille, send the notarized document with a self-addressed envelope, check made payable to the Treasurer, State of N.J. and forwarded to The Dept. of Treasury. Notary Section, P.O.B. 452, Trenton, N.J. 08646; Call 609.292.9292, for the fee amount.

Authentication/Legalization of Notary Commission

Anyone can make a request from the State Treasurer or County Clerk where the Oath was taken, for verification of signature. A seal is attached to an acknowledgement or jurat as genuine. Also, the Notary has authority to act at the time of the notarization. N.J.S.A. 52:7-15

County Clerk's office will attach a certificate of proof, acknowledgements or affidavits. N.J.S.A. 52:7-16

It is not the Notary's responsibility to request an authenticating certificate for a signers notarized document. (N.N.A.)

Protests For Non-Payment/Non-Acceptance: NJSA 2A:82:7

Protest is a formal declaration made by the Notary on behalf of a holder of a bill or note that acceptance or payment of the bill/note has been refused. *Due to advancement of technology in the banking industry this is rarely used if at all.*

N.J.S.A. 7:5-3 Record of Protest Journal is addressed here referencing: Recording date – time – where – whom – demand for payment – when served – etc. Common sense procedures perhaps referencing this statute in strongly suggesting Notaries use a JOURNAL.

N.J.S.A. 7:5-5 Death or Removal of notary; deposit of record As previously suggested in Record of Protest procedures are strongly suggesting "Notaries deposit this record with the office of the clerk of the county in which last resided".

OPENING SAFE DEPOSIT BOXES
N.J. Statute up dated 02.14.2012 reference NJSA17:14A-51-71

The procedure for unpaid rentals: If safe deposit box goes unpaid after the expiration of one year, the financial institute can send a written notice by registered mail, addressed to the lessee/lessees name on the rental agreement.

If not responded to within 30 days from the date of the letter the institute will have the safety deposit opened in the presence of: an Officer, Notary Public not employed by the financial institute, and a locksmith. (N.J.S.A. 17:14A-51)

Opening a Safety Deposit Box

State of: New Jersey   <   WHERE YOUR FEET ARE PLANTED   >   County of: Ocean

On this _____ day of _____ 20_____ safe deposit box number (s) _____ , rented in the name (s) of

_____

was/were opened in the presence of the undersigned. The contents of the box(s) consisted of the following: _____

_____

_____   _____
^ Bank Officer Signature   ^ Notary Signature

_____   _____
^ Print Bank Officer Name   ^ Print Notary Name and expiration date

_____
^ Locksmith Signature

_____
^ Print Locksmith Name
                                                                  SEAL
_____
^ Print Locksmith Company Name

MY NOTES:

_____

_____

_____

_____

_____

_____

_____

MY NOTES: Section 3

Section 4
Tips For The Notary Public

KNOWLEDGE IS POWER

❑ Contents of the document "should be reviewed" for completeness meaning no blank spaces. Call to the attention of the signer. Signer should line through or N/A and initial. Do NOT notarize incomplete documents.
❑ The Notary and the Signer MUST be able to communicate.
❑ The Notary must verbalize what the document is to make certain that the signer knows what "is being signed". Also, to record NOTARIZED documents in your Journal.

✓ The date on the Notarial Certificate is the date the individual appears before the Notary Public and the document is sealed.
✓ The date of the document does not necessarily matter to the notary. The date should be prior to the notarization. NEVER FOLLOWING THE DATE OF THE NOTARIZTION.
✓ The Notary NEVER BACK DATES OR POST DATES A NOTARIAL CERTIFICATE. Doing so is fraudulent and there is NO legal defense.
✓ Know and study N.J. Statutes for Notaries.
✓ NEVER – NEVER – JUST "SIGN & STAMP"
✓ ALWAYS – MUST HAVE: VENUE – TEXT – SIGNATURE – DATE OF APPEARANCE & SIGNING – EXPIRATION DATE – PRINTED NAME

My Notes:

_____

_____

_____

_____

_____

_____

GETTING STARTED

Your First Assignment

Good habits keep the Notary Public out of trouble. From day one set a routine and follow it. What works for us: Informing signers of your requirements before appointment:

<u>Photo I.D. preferably D/L and/or Passport</u>

1. First advise the signer(s) what you are going to do and how you are doing it. Advising signer(s) importance of journal.
    a. Recording I.D. in Journal.
    b. Record documents being notarized and pages.
    c. Request for their signature and thumbprint.
    d. Informing them you give an Oath and Acknowledgement.
    e. Ask the signer(s) If they have any questions?
2. Good time for some PR…Public Relations…. If signers refuse and/or question something, explain why you do what you do. Take all the time necessary to educate the public. If the question is the fingerprint…..explain that it is not the law YET, but it is the best form of I.D. should a problem come up in the future. EX. Questioning who was at the table.
3. Proceed with official signing.

MY NOTES:

_____

_____

_____

_____

_____

_____

Following Completion

- ❑ Review the document presented for completeness.
- ❑ This is not a formal legal review, such as, would be performed by an accountant or an attorney.
- ❑ Rather, it is a review to ensure that there are no blanks in the document.
- ❑ Should blanks be discovered, the signer must either fill them in or strike them out by drawing a line or "X" through them or N/A, good idea to initial.
- ❑ To not fill in the blanks is dangerous; not good business practice; violation of common sense; liken to signing a blank check. A falsified document could be attached in its place.
- ❑ Check and recheck your documents at the table for missed – signatures – initials – stamp – blanks – etc.
- ❑ REMINDER: Review your Notarizations as well for completeness.

SUPPORT – CONTACT – SUPPLIES

Valuable Contact Information

General Information:
Office of Legislative Services,
Office of Public Information
Room 50; State House Annex
P.O. Box 068;
Trenton, NJ 08625-0068

Phone: (609) 292-4840 - Toll Free (800) 792-8630
TDD: (609) 777-2744 - Toll Free (800) 257-7490

OFFICE OF PUBLIC INFORMATION   **www.njleg.state.nj.us**

Contact information for the
NJ Dept. of State
Division of Commercial Recording;
Notary Public Section - N.J.N.P. Manual
P.O. Box 452 - Trenton, NJ 08625
1-609-292-9292

www.state.nj.us/treasury/revenue/dcr/geninfo/notary manual.htm

N.J.N.P. 1979 Statutes

http://cdn.nationalnotary.org/nna_members/state_law_summaries/new_jersey.pdf

American Society of Notaries,
P.O. Box 5707, Tallahassee, Fl. 32314-5707
Phone: 1.850.671.5164
Web Site: www.asnnotary.org

Notary Supplies
http://www.asnnotary.org/img/ASN%202012%20Notary%20Supply%20Catalog.pdf

MEMBERSHIP
http://www.asnnotary.org/?form=membership

Resources

The State of N.J. recommends the following reading and/or research books:
- **New Jersey Notary Handbook –   American Society of Notaries**
- **The N.J. Notary Law Primer   National Notary Association**
- **A Guide for New Jersey . East Coast Publishing, Poughkeepsie, NY, 1991. Piambino**
- **Notary Public Handbook, Wesley, Gilmer.**
- **Anderson's Manual for Notaries Public.6th Ed. Anderson Publishing Co. Cincinnati, OH. 1991.**
- **Kessinger, Roger A. Notary Public Handbook: A State-by-State Guide. Kessinger Publishing Col. Boise, ID, 1990.**
- **Van Alstyne's Notary Public Encyclopedia. America's most Comprehensive Reference Source on Notary Public Principles.**

Various websites – however, be careful sometimes info may be clouded. Check several sources. Call your notary membership hotlines.
National Notary Society:

http://cdn.nationalnotary.org/resources_for_notaries/Notary_Code.pdf

http://www.nationalnotary.org/reference_material_and_publications/model_notary_act/index.html

Section 5
The New Notary Public
THE PRO-ACTIVE NOTARY PUBLIC

- ➢ Reads the N.J. Notary Manual.
- ➢ READS & Prints "OPINION 41".
- ➢ Uses resources – contact information provided.
- ➢ Has a Notary Public Organization membership.
- ➢ Takes out an E&O policy.
- ➢ Understands the different purpose for:
    - ➢ a. Acknowledgement
    - ➢ b. Jurat
    - ➢ c. Affidavit

MY NOTES: Section 4 & 5 Plus other…..

_____

_____

_____

_____

_____

_____

_____

_____

_____

_____

_____

_____

_____

_____

_____

_____

_____

_____

_____

_____

SAMPLE

All Purpose Acknowledgement

State of: New Jersey
County of:

On this _____ day of _____, 2011 before me _____

a Notary Public, personally appeared _____

_____, personally known to me OR proved to me
on the basis of satisfactory evidence to be the person/persons whose name/names is/are subscribed
to the within instrument and acknowledged to me that he/she/they executed the same in
his/her/their authorized capacity/capacities, and that by his/her/their signature/signatures on the
instrument the person/persons acted, executed this instrument.

Witness my hand and seal   _____,
                                  ^Notary Signature   <Notary Printed Name
                                  My Commission Expires: _____

(Seal)

SAMPLE

Jurat

State of _____   County of_____

On this, the _____ day of _____, 20____, before me, _____, the undersigned officer, personally appeared _____, (known to me) or (proven by satisfactory evidence) or ((proved to me on the oath or affirmation of _____ who is personally known to me) or (proved by satisfactory evidence and stated to me that he/she/they know the document signer and are unaffected by the document)), to be the person(s) who's name(s) is/are subscribed to the within instrument, who signed the preceding or attached document in my presence and who swore or affirmed to me that the contents of the document are truthful and accurate to the best of his/her/their knowledge and belief.

In witness whereof, I hereunto set my hand and official seal.

Witness my hand and seal:

_____,
^Notary Signature   <Notary Printed Name
My Commission Expires: _____

(Seal)

S A M P L E

Affidavit Certificate

State of: New Jersey
County of:

I, _____ (Affiant), make the following sworn statement:
_____
_____
_____
_____
_____
_____
_____

_____
^ Affiant Signature   <Printed Name

Subscribed and sworn or affirmed before me by _____, **this**
_____ **day of** _____, 20_____.

Witness my hand and seal:

_____,
^Notary Signature   <Notary Printed Name

My Commission Expires: _____

(Seal)

ATLANTIC County Clerk's Office 5901 Main Street Mays Landing, NJ 08330 **609- 625-4011 X 5242** (FAX) 609-909-5111	BERGEN County Clerk's Office One Bergen County Plaza Room 122 Hackensack, NJ 07601 **201-336-7006** (FAX) 201-336-7002	BURLINGTON County Clerk's Office Courts Building, First Floor 49 Rancocas Road Mount Holly, NJ 08060 **609-265-5122** (FAX) 609-265-0696
CAMDEN County Clerk's Office 520 Market Street, Room 102 hours: 8:30-4:00 P.M. Camden, NJ 08102 **856-225-5324** (FAX) 856-225-5316	CAPE MAY County Clerk's Office 7 N. Main Street, P.O. Box 5000 Cape May Courthouse, NJ 08210 **609-465-1010** (FAX) 609-465-8625 ccclerk@co.cape-may.NJ.US	CUMBERLAND County Clerk's Off. 60 W. Broad Street, RM A137 Bridgeton, NJ 08302 **856 453 4861** (FAX) 856-455-1410
ESSEX County Clerk's Office 465 Martin Luther King Blvd. Room 247 Newark, NJ 07102-0690 **973-621-4921** *(for regular mail delivery use P.O.* *Box 690, Newark, NJ 07101-* *0690)*	GLOUCESTER County Clerk's Office Old Court House, 1st Floor 1 North Broad Street Woodbury, NJ 08096 **856-853-3241** (FAX) 856-853-3327	HUDSON County Clerk's Office Hudson City Plaza, 4th Floor 257 Cornelison Avenue Jersey City, NJ 07302 **201-369-3470 X 2756** countyclerk@hcnj.us
HUNTERDON County Clerk's Office 71 Main Street P.O. Box 2900 Hall of Records Flemington, NJ 08822 **908-788-1214** (FAX) 908-782-4068 countyclerk@co.hunterdon.nj.us	MERCER County Clerk's Office Court House, P.O. Box 8068 209 S. Broad Street Trenton, NJ 08650-0068 **609-989-6465** (FAX) 609-989-1111	MIDDLESEX County Clerk's Office 75 Bayard Street New Brunswick, NJ 08901 **732-745-3197** (FAX) 732-745-3642
MONMOUTH County Clerk's Office 33 Mechanic Street Freehold, NJ 07728 **732-683-8743** (FAX) 732-409-7566	MORRIS County Clerk's Office Hall of Records-Administration Bldg. Morristown, NJ 07963 **973-285-6120** (FAX) 973-285-6171	OCEAN County Clerk's Office P.O. Box 2191 118 Washington Street Toms River, NJ 08754 **732-929-2018** (FAX) 732-349-4336
PASSAIC County Clerk's Office 401 Grand Street Room 130 Paterson, NJ 07505 **973-225-3632 X 300** (FAX) 973-754-1920	SALEM County Clerk's Office 92 Market Street Salem, NJ 08079 **856-339-8605** (FAX) 856-935-8882	SOMERSET County Clerk's Office P.O. Box 3000 Somerville, NJ 08876 **908-231-7017** (FAX) 908-725-3012
SUSSEX County Clerk's Office Hall of Records 83 Spring Street, Suite 304 Newton, NJ 07860 **973-579-0900** (FAX) 973-383-7493 ccclerk@nac.net	UNION County Clerk's Office Court House Union City 2 Broad Street, RM 115 Elizabeth, NJ 07207 **908-527-4789** (FAX) 908-558-2589	WARREN County Clerk's Office 413 Second Street Belvidere, NJ 07823 **908-475-6215** (FAX) 908-475-6208

Printed in the United States
By Bookmasters